FIFTY FASHION LOOKS THAT CHANGED THE 1980s

**DESIGN
MUSEUM**

FIFTY FASHION LOOKS
THAT CHANGED THE 1980s

**PAULA
REED**

conran
OCTOPUS

THE
1980s

Diana, Princess of Wales, was undoubtedly the style icon of the 1980s, as she transformed from archetypal Sloane Ranger to sophisticated fashion leader.

Above: Ska girls in Coventry, UK, in 1980. The ska sound and look started its third revival at about this time. Below: The now-ubiquitous phenomenon of the Amazonian supermodel first developed in the late 1980s.

THE
1980s

Nineteen eighty-one: in Britain, the wedding of Lady Diana Spencer and Charles, Prince of Wales, and in America, the arrival of Ronald and Nancy Reagan in the White House, were the catalysts for fashion to pursue luxury and romance. It would be the decade of power dressing but also the decade of subversion. The triumph of greed in the boardroom would be countered by a riotous energy in the streets.

In terms of fashion, if the 1960s belonged to London and the 1970s to New York, Paris seemed determined to claim the 1980s. It was a creative free-for-all. The catwalks reflected the exuberance of a time when everything was entirely possible and there were no creative restraints. The arrival of the Japanese, however, offered a more cerebral alternative to the glamorous French, sexy Italians and subversive British.

Shows took place in vast tents, not salons, and were no longer the reserve of the industry insider. They were events that were mobbed by fans and hangers-on, and people fought for a place among the audience. The Dé d'or (Golden Thimble) or French 'Fashion Oscars' were broadcast from the Palais Garnier. The new wave achieved equal footing with old-style couture.

The unpalatable reality of this new-found success was that it forced designers to learn to be businessmen and -women. Between the creativity and carousing there were fortunes to be made. The fashion world lost its nonchalance and became increasingly commercial. Fashion had become big business.

Some of the big names in 1980s British fashion assemble to promote Fashion Aid, including David and Elizabeth Emanuel, Scott Crolla, Jerry Hall, Katharine Hamnett, Bruce Oldfield and Jasper Conran. It is an image that captures something of the eclecticism and brashness of the decade.

DALLAS AND *DYNASTY*

Never knowingly under-accessorized

The soap operas *Dallas* and *Dynasty* were the must-see TV of the 1980s. Throughout the decade they jockeyed for position in a ratings war that attracted global audiences of over 250 million. They tuned in for the bitchy asides ('Take your blonde tramp and get out of my house!' – Alexis Colby); they tuned in for the cat fights (Alexis vs. Krystle in *Dynasty* and Sue Ellen vs. Pamela Ewing in *Dallas*), but mostly they tuned in for the hairdos and clothes.

Even though Sue Ellen Ewing ran her own fashion line in *Dallas*, *Dynasty* had the undoubted fashion edge. The costume designer Nolan Miller was inundated with letters and calls inquiring about the *Dynasty* stars' wardrobes. Linda Evans's broad shoulders and Nolan Miller's designer vision evolved into the wasp-waisted power suit of the 1980s. Embellishments such as lace, brocade, fur and jewels elaborated the angular shape of the shoulder-padded silhouette.

The *Dynasty* women were never knowingly under-accessorized. Liberal helpings of statement costume jewellery were worn day and night by the show's female stars and drifted into mainstream fashion. Big gilt fashion earrings, several centimetres across, drew attention to faces bobbing above shoulder pads and under waves of moussed and lacquered hair. Eveningwear was Miller's forte. Column gowns with intricate details played to the characters' archetypes: Krystle typically wore an understated palette of whites, creams and beiges; Alexis, on the other hand, favoured scarlet and blacks.

Miller's *Dynasty* collection was launched in New York's Bloomingdale's in 1984. The surge of 20,000 covetous fans forced management to temporarily close the doors. Miller attributed the success of the line to the characters' undeniable élan. 'I don't think any other show has ever concentrated … on the look.'

Dallas (below) and *Dynasty* (right) were set in an era when the *ne plus ultra* was to be rich, resplendent in shoulder pads worthy of a line backer and blessed with a head of hair that could be whipped up to gravity-defying heights.

DONNA KARAN

Woman-friendly fashion

Donna Karan's (1948–) fashion concept was built around the idea of a man's wardrobe – tops and bottoms rather than outfits. Women fell in love with the Karan staples: a slim dress, a wrap skirt, easy-cut trousers, a sharp-shouldered jacket and, of course, the body suit – a fitted base layer that snapped into the crotch so that it never came untucked or looked messy. 'The Body' became perhaps the decade's single most copied item of clothing.

Karan's fuss-free approach put her firmly in the fashion family of Alaïa, Zoran and Claire McCardell. She offered uncomplicated, sexy wearability – clothes that would 'travel, interchange and impress'. With the addition of her sculptural jewellery, designed by Robert Lee Morris of Artwear, a few Donna Karan pieces could take her customer from work to play – the concept of day to evening dressing was born here.

Her designs were slimming and flattering. Her gathered skirts hid the tummy while her wedge-shaped dresses made women look taller. And women swore by her hosiery. Fortified by Lycra, her tights were a breakthrough that made women's legs look longer and slimmer, and every hosiery manufacturer rushed to copy them. In 1989 Karan spawned another winner with the DKNY line which became a 100-million-dollar business in its first year.

'I design from my guts,' said Karen, describing her no-brainer approach. 'Before every season I open up my closet and see what's missing. Then I design what I want to wear.'

Donna Karan (with the designer Louis Dell'Olio) in 1980. The Donna Karan woman could afford to wear the designer creations of Bill Blass or Oscar de la Renta, but high-powered baby-boomers wanted a designer from their own generation.

GRACE JONES AND JEAN-PAUL GOUDE

The image makers

In the early 1970s, along with Jerry Hall, Iman and Pat Cleveland, Grace Jones (1948–) ruled over the glamorous dominions of the New York club scene and Paris catwalks. With her fine features (you could lacerate yourself on those cheeks, affectionately known in the industry as the 'Jones Bones') and athletic body, she rapidly became fashion's most sought-after black model. She began singing in 1977, subsequently signing for Island Records, where initially her contribution to popular music amounted to not much more than a series of dance tracks, played mainly in gay discos. Then she met the art director Jean-Paul Goude (1940–).

Together, Goude and Jones worked on hundreds of portraits of Grace, playing with her proportions and her sexuality in a variety of colourful and subversive images that usually involved montage or photorealist techniques. The result was the reinvention of Grace as 'the first black new wave artist'. They amped up her startling attributes: adding wide-shouldered men's Armani jackets, developing a robotic way of dancing and capitalizing on that raspy drawl. One of the most startling things about the reimagined Grace was her magnificent flat top (which had begun life on Goude's drawing board) – a haircut of head-turning geometric uniqueness.

Grace Jones in a 'Constructivist' maternity dress designed in collaboration with the fashion illustrator Antonio Lopez. Together, Jones, Goude and Lopez created one of the most powerful pop presences of the decade.

PRADA BLACK NYLON BAG

The first 'IT' bag

Prada had begun life as Fratelli Prada, a shop in the fashionable Galleria Vittorio Emanuele in Milan selling Italian leather goods and imported English steamer trunks. Miuccia Prada (1949–), with a doctorate in political science and a passion for women's rights, was an unlikely choice to run a luggage shop. Nevertheless, in 1978 she took over the family business from her mother.

Her business partner was her new husband, Patrizio Bertelli, who took care of the business while she set about reinventing the product. They had entirely different but complementary skills. But both Miuccia and Patrizio were entirely in agreement about one important thing: to market Prada using its *lack* of prestigious appeal, capitalizing on 'anti-status' and 'reverse snobbery'. The timing, just as fashion began to tire of conspicuous consumption, was bang on the zeitgeist. Together they would transform the family firm into a global fashion powerhouse.

It made sense for a purveyor of luggage to develop an accessories range first. From early versions developed at the beginning of the decade, the chicly understated but eminently practical bags became a cult hit among fashion insiders: the models and photographers who commuted between Milan, Paris, London and New York. They were made out of utilitarian black nylon: first, the heavy-duty stuff that her grandfather had used for the protective covers of his steamer trunks and, later, a more practical nylon twill that was developed specially for the purpose.

It would take only four years for Prada to have enough of a war chest to launch a ready-to-wear collection, the clothing reflecting the same knack for classic understatement as the accessories.

The power of understatement in the decade of excess – the Prada black nylon bag.

RALPH LAUREN
A world of luxury

Once a shadowy figure behind the label, the 1980s saw 'the designer' emerging to make videos and in-store appearances, to take top table at charity galas and, of course, to feature in their own advertising campaigns. First among these was Ralph Lauren (born Ralph Lifshitz in 1939). In 1981 a seven-spread advertisement in British *Vogue,* introducing the Polo store in London's Bond Street, opened with a full-page picture of the billionaire designer himself, clad in his signature denims and cowboy belt.

Lauren's philosophy, however, was not so much about self-aggrandizement as his innate understanding that modern fashion was about inclusion – about belonging to a world or lifestyle that felt good, looked good and, above all, was accessible. Like the American Dream, fashion had to appear available to all, regardless of the economic reality in which people lived. He also passionately believed in the marketable appeal of American style. 'The American sensibility has become a very important international sensibility,' he said. 'We created sportswear. Ours is a more modern culture because of the way we live. We travel, we're athletic, we move.'

In 1986 Ralph Lauren opened his New York flagship store in the elegant Rhinelander Mansion on Madison Avenue, creating retail's most sumptuous *mise-en-scène*. With Cole Porter tunes drifting through the air, it was easy to get carried away – as millions of Americans and tourists did, trooping home with armloads of Polo shopping bags.

Ralph Lauren discussing fashion direction with fitting model Lynn Yeager, at his Seventh Avenue studio in Manhattan in 1980. Lauren's clothes epitomized the American Dream – aspirational and accessible.

BRIDESHEAD REVISITED

Small-screen chic

The must-see TV of the decade was an extravagantly stylish series of 11 episodes that cost a splashy £11 million, was previewed in all the fashion magazines and, in TV terms, has remained unrivalled both for viewing figures and fashion influence until the arrival of *Downton Abbey* in 2010. *Brideshead Revisited*, an epic adaptation of Evelyn Waugh's 1945 novel about the decline and fall of an English aristocratic family in the 1920s and '30s, starred Jeremy Irons as Charles Ryder, Anthony Andrews as Sebastian Flyte (along with Aloysius the bear), Diana Quick as Julia Flyte, Claire Bloom as Lady Marchmain and Sir Laurence Olivier as Lord Marchmain. The series also featured the city of Oxford as itself, and Castle Howard as Brideshead, the Marchmain family seat.

The clothes were as articulate as the script in portraying the nuances of a socially stratified time. Costume designer Jane Robinson skilfully managed to portray Flyte's social dexterity and Ryder's awkwardness by choosing impeccably tailored suits for the one and rather less stylish jackets and trousers for the other. Ryder's wardrobe, of course, evolves as he absorbs some of the sartorial smoothness of his aristocratic friend, and by the time they reach Venice in the second episode he is wearing his cream linen suits and tying his silk ascots with impressive ease. Diana Quick's wardrobe inspired summers of dropped waists, cloche hats and fringed oriental shawls wherever the series was broadcast.

Waugh was aware of the visual drama of the book: 'I am writing a very beautiful book, to bring tears, about very rich, beautiful people, who live in palaces and have no troubles except what they make themselves…'

The *Brideshead* look unleashed a wave of nostalgic fashions, from drop-waisted flapper dresses and shawls to knitted tank tops and impeccable linen suits.

NANCY REAGAN

First Lady in red

In 1981 *Newsweek* ran a story with the headline 'Mrs. Reagan's Free Clothes' in which it was alleged that Nancy Reagan had accepted an unspecified number of gowns, jewels and gifts from top designers. By December that year a poll conducted for the same publication found that 62 per cent of the American public thought Nancy Reagan (1921–) put 'too much emphasis on style'. If it seemed unfair that Mrs Reagan was criticized for the very qualities that had been deemed admirable in Mrs Kennedy, it is worth remembering that the country was in recession and that central to Reaganomics were savage Federal budget cuts.

'Queen Nancy', as she was dubbed, was the poster girl of the charity ball set – for whom ostentation was the oxygen of social success. By the early 1980s the Arab ladies who lined the pockets of couturiers in the 1970s had been joined on their shopping trips by the Americans. The Reagan-era 'ladies who lunched' – women like Ivana Trump, Nan Kempner, Ann Getty, Pat Buckley and Lynn Wyatt – all headed to the Paris couture shows by Concorde, were known never to wear the same outfit twice, and happily blew $100,000 or more on a couture wardrobe in a single trip.

In her couture gowns from favourite designers Oscar de la Renta, Galanos, Adolfo and Bill Blass, Nancy Reagan presided over a set of world-class party-goers and -givers. Her white, hand-beaded, one-shoulder Galanos gown, worn for her husband's inauguration, was estimated to cost $10,000, while the overall price of her inaugural wardrobe was said to cost $25,000.

The official portrait from 1981. Nancy Reagan had a preference for red, which she called her 'picker-upper', and wore it until it became her style signature. In fact, her wardrobe included red so often that the fire-engine shade even became known as 'Reagan red'.

VIVIENNE WESTWOOD, 'PIRATES'

1981

Dressing up punk

The cusp of the 1980s marked a turning point for Vivienne Westwood (1941–) as she switched her focus from the street to the salon and began her campaign to revolutionize fashion. The 'Pirates' collection of Autumn/Winter 1981–82 created a romantic unisex landscape inhabited by buccaneers and dandies. She changed the name and ambience of her New Kings Road boutique to match, transforming its interior into the cabin of an ocean-roving galleon and rechristening it 'World's End'.

After separating from Malcolm McLaren in 1983, Westwood began to build on a style of startling originality, often based on contemporary reworkings of traditional garments. Her 'Mini-Crini' collection of Spring/Summer 1985 was an impertinent reinterpretation of demure Victoriana. The corseted cut of her suits and shirts thrust the bust forward (spilling over 'like milk jellies', she said), nipped in the waist and arched the back and hips. High waists and shoulders free of padding reintroduced Regency swagger. Her 'Harris Tweed' collection of Autumn/Winter 1987–88 dusted off the wardrobe staples of the seventeenth century.

Westwood inspired respect and astonishment in equal measures. Audiences were dazzled as much by her technical skill as by her creative excess. Her goal was no less than a cultural revolution: 'It is an artist's job to wreak violence on a culture to give it new life … My aim is to make the poor look rich and the rich look poor.' She was unique among designers as someone who consistently justified what she did in broad cultural terms.

Model Lizzie Tear wearing the 'Pirates' look outside Westwood's World's End store. The plundering of the dressing-up box of historical fashion styles was to be the hallmark of the designer through the decade and beyond.

THE STYLE PRESS

New fashion bibles

There was a time when fashion was for those who could afford it and fashion magazines were symbols of wealth and unaffordable taste. Punk brought fashion down from the catwalk and onto the streets, taking the establishment by surprise. And it spawned a shelfful of magazines so caught up in the minutiae and evolution of every new trend that they were more than mere style magazines – they were style *bibles*.

Blitz magazine (published 1980–91) enabled stylists such as Kim Bowen and Iain R. Webb, flamboyant regulars at its namesake club, to express themselves on paper. Nick Logan's magazine *The Face* (1980–2004) led the field with radical art direction and innovative fonts by designer Neville Brody. Terry Jones's *i-D* (1980–) was originally a stapled fanzine, but evolved into a style magazine with a radical agenda. It featured the opinions of 'ordinary' young people – their taste in music and fashion and their political opinions.

Street fashion was at the heart of all of these magazines. A flagging economy and rising unemployment were the backdrops for a burgeoning music and media industry. As a form of self-expression, street fashion thrived in the clubs and art colleges of Britain. And the style press gave it a voice.

A cover from an early edition of *The Face* showing the New Romantic pop trio the Human League. *The Face* was part of a new wave in magazine publishing that helped bring 'image' into the mainstream.

THE FACE

NUMBER 17   SEPTEMBER 1981   65p
EIRE 91p (inc. VAT)

HUMAN LEAGUE

PHOTO: JILL FURMANOVSKY

IAN DURY
SLY & ROBBIE
CABARET VOLTAIRE
OK JIVE
JAH WOBBLE

VISIONS OF THE VIDEO AGE: Special Report
TATTOOS: The Mark of the Outsider?
STYLE: The Beat Goes On/History of the Zoot Suit

BRUCE WEBER

Fashion's all-American

1982

It was Bruce Weber (1946–) who provided one of the most influential and controversial contributions to fashion photography, through his portfolios for *Vogue* and advertising campaigns that helped make commercial giants of the American brands Ralph Lauren and Calvin Klein. He carved a niche for himself as cheerleader for the All-American fashion story. The defining theme, in all of his work, is the freckle-faced spirit of hearty outdoor leisure and simple romance. He was the supreme creator of fantasy at a time when fashion's obsession with the impeccably art-directed lifestyle was gathering momentum.

Typically, he would take a group of friends and stars to a remote spot on the map and photograph them over the course of a few days, producing pictures that had the intimacy and reality of a family album. Weber's subjects never really looked posed. They were often shot leaping off wooden docks into gleaming Adirondack lakes or engaged in wholesome pursuits such as lacrosse, soccer or surfing. He sought not so much to sell clothes as to project an image and a personality. The clothes were often secondary to the portraits and often at the mercy of the casual treatment meted out to them by the models.

Weber's Calvin Klein advertisements were hugely influential in the fashion industry but also highly controversial. The value of his work was often hotly debated or, as was frequently the case in the 1980s, decried – much along the same lines as the homoerotic photographs of Robert Mapplethorpe.

The Olympic pole vaulter Tom Hintnaus appears on an enormous billboard in New York City's Times Square wearing nothing but his bikini brief. Weber's work for Calvin Klein, with its unabashed celebration (and commercialization) of the male body, was a startling innovation at the time.

Calvin Klein Underwear

Portable Component System.

JVC

BROADWAY

ONE WAY

QUALITY AUD

GIORGIO ARMANI

Italian ease

In 1975 Giorgio Armani (1934–) opened his fashion house with a radically chic look – the unconstructed suit, which blurred the distinction between business and casual, and whose supple materials draped and rumpled gracefully. Then, in 1980, in the movie *American Gigolo*, Richard Gere was a walking Armani fashion show, putting the designer on the Hollywood fashion radar and soon making him one of the world's best-selling designers.

From Wall Street to West Hollywood, men of all pinstripes got into the Armani habit. The designer – who had spent an impoverished childhood in postwar Piacenza, started his career as a window dresser at La Rinascente department store in Milan, and found the money to start his company only by selling his Volkswagen Beetle – cast the same spell over a new generation of executive women who were unimpressed with the fussy figure-compressing haute couture coming out of Paris. Armani's soft, comfortable tailoring was a runaway hit in the feminist age.

The centrepiece of Armani's celebrity strategy was the Academy Awards, the biggest photo opportunity of the year. After Armani opened his Beverly Hills boutique in 1988, he single-mindedly set out to become the designer of choice on Oscar Night, and he succeeded. By 1991 *WWD* (*Women's Wear Daily*) was calling the Oscars 'The Armani Awards': the designer would forever be remembered as the first to sweep the Oscars without taking home a single trophy.

Giorgio Armani and models. For men and women alike, the Armani suit became the pinnacle of power dressing. Rosita Missoni told *Women's Wear Daily*, 'Armani put women in men's clothes. He is a genius.'

ISSEY MIYAKE
East greets West

Issey Miyake (1938–) was a survivor of the atomic bomb in Hiroshima. He studied graphic design at the Tama Art University in Tokyo, before moving to Europe to serve apprenticeships with couturiers Guy Laroche and Hubert de Givenchy. He followed with a stint at the right hand of Geoffrey Beene in New York. In 1973 he showed his first collection in Paris and, along with Kenzo Takada, blazed a trail for the later arrival of other Japanese designers such as Yamamoto, Matsuda and Kawakubo. Collectively, they exerted a seismic influence on the avant-garde aesthetic of the 1980s.

While Kenzo worked in the European fashion vernacular, Miyake offered the East to the West in a singularly undiluted form. He maintained a base in Japan and an unmistakably Japanese feel to his clothes. Concentrating on fluidity and texture, he combined these with the professional techniques he had honed in the studios of Laroche, Givenchy and Beene. Miyake allied traditional Eastern styles, materials, colours and skills, such a sashiko quilting, with ultramodern techniques of manufacture, to create loose comfortable clothes.

Throughout the 1980s Miyake pursued his exploration of new ways of dressing the body, while collaboration with Japanese textile manufacturers enabled him to create uniquely innovative fabrics. In the 1980s he invented a concept that allowed a hot press to pleat a garment permanently after it was cut and sewn. It was a technique that proved so popular that it led to the launch of the Pleats Please label in 1993.

A shot from Miyake's ready-to-wear show, Spring/Summer 1982. The designer's cool colour palette and loose fluid structures were seen by some as a badly needed corrective to the overstated styles of the 1980s.

NEW ROMANTICS

Perfectly posed pop

On the cusp of the new decade, the phenomenon we now call the 'New Romantics' was born at the Blitz Club, in London's Covent Garden. The establishment closed in 1981 but by then had already spawned a generation of poseurs who helped define the 1980s. Among the 'Blitz Kids' were Steve Strange, Boy George, Stephen Jones, Kim Bowen, Stephen Linard, Fiona Dealey, David Holah, Stevie Stewart, Julia Fodor, Willie Brown, Chris Sullivan, Judith Franklin and Darla Jane Gilroy. They made their first appearance en masse at the Saint Martins School of Art's Alternative Fashion Show, which featured a catwalk appearance by Boy George.

The New Romantics scrambled codes so much that at first people had difficulty labelling this brash new youth cult, but 'Peacock Punks' and 'Blitz Kids' were eventually discarded in favour of 'New Romantics'. The age of plunder had arrived and, as period dress became fashionable, Britain experienced a style revolution as past, present and future, sex and gender, were all mashed up into one big kaleidoscopic potpourri. This was skip culture where something old, something new and something borrowed were all used to create the emperor's new clothes.

Whatever talents Steve Strange and (Boy) George O'Dowd had for courting publicity, they were entirely dependent on their elite corps of sharp-eyed trendsetters to create the clothes that defined their idiosyncratic and ever-mutating identities. Image was all important, and soon pop stars began to furiously reinvent themselves, as everyone did the resurrection shuffle.

The British New Romantic band Duran Duran in the early 1980s. The Blitz generation took punk and dressed it up, gave it a 12-inch dance remix and styled its hair.

STATUS DRESSING

Fashion goes bling

As a new age of wealth and conservatism dawned, the love affair of the newly rich with status dressing blossomed. The *grandes maisons* of luxury embarked on a boom that was to last uninterrupted for the next decade. The price of ready-to-wear rose and so did the numbers of women who lusted after it. Haute couture – the apex of luxury fashion and traditionally the reserve of the aged and uber-wealthy bourgeoisie – attracted a burgeoning clientele of younger women. The average age was between 25 and 35, and almost half were American.

Christian Lacroix at Patou, Eric Bergère at Hermès and Karl Lagerfeld at Chanel (see page 80) particularly appealed to this market. Luxurious party frocks that came in at the same price as suburban homes became the badge of wealthy Arab ladies, trophy wives and international socialites. Hermès surfed the wave of status dressing: Grace Kelly twinsets, silk scarves and oversize 'Kelly bags' at £1,000 a time were sell-out items. Ironically, only a few years before, Hermès had struggled to sell a single one of what has now become one of the great iconic handbags.

Designer labels gained a new-found power. Brand names became status symbols to covet and show off and were applied to goods as varied as sports gear, perfumes, luggage and sunglasses. The new rich, it seemed, did not want so much to consume as to be *seen* to consume.

Conspicuous wealth: model Kelly Emberg leans against a luggage cart at an airport, surrounded by pilots and wearing clothes by Calvin Klein, with a red quilted bag by Chanel, a brown leather shoulder bag by Mark Cross, and pullman bags by Lancel.

In terms of tabloid handles, 'Million Dollar Faces' does not have quite the same ring as 'supermodels', but in 1981 this is what *Life* magazine called a new generation of highly paid models that included Lauren Hutton, Iman, Margaux Hemingway, Janice Dickinson and Cheryl Tiegs. Glossy magazine covers, swimsuit spreads in *Sports Illustrated*, six-figure cosmetics contracts and the inevitable marriage to a rock star: the potent combination of beauty and fame ensured that this new breed was able to endorse anything from diet drinks to pick-up trucks.

The era of the supermodel may have been in its infancy but these ladies were trailblazers in the land of big bucks. Early in the decade, Inès de la Fressange became the exclusive face of Karl Lagerfeld's Chanel. Carol Alt, Kim Alexis and Christie Brinkley were the power triumvirate of print, dominating *Vogue* and *Sports Illustrated* covers throughout the decade.

Gia Carangi (1960–86) was, for a time, the model's model. A favourite of Helmut Newton, she could express the haughty exclusivity of couture and yet had enough of the common touch to make her commercially successful, too. Her career spiralled out of control owing to her heroin addiction. Iman (1955–) is another icon of the decade: an example of how to live quietly but still maintain your fame. The Somalian-born model was cited as a muse by designers including Halston, Calvin Klein and Yves Saint Laurent. She was the queen of the catwalk, a model of mesmerizing elegance.

Such was the power and presence of these women that gradually models started to move in on the glamorous and seductive territory that was the traditional reserve of the movie star. Their success transcended the catwalk and magazine covers. They built careers based not so much on their talent as individuals but on the power of their images.

Portrait of American model Janice Dickinson during a photoshoot for Italian *Vogue*, in 1983.

DIANA, PRINCESS OF WALES

Reinventing royalty

It was Diana, Princess of Wales (1961–97), who set a style of easy, youthful elegance for a new royal generation and became the star of the decade.

Her public debut, her wedding to Prince Charles in 1981, was conducted before a worldwide television audience of 750 million viewers. The silk taffeta wedding dress, designed by David and Elizabeth Emanuel, studded with 10,000 pearls and decorated with Carrickmacross lace, was of such billowing proportions that it made it difficult for Diana's father to accompany her in the glass coach to Westminster Abbey. 'Too much dress; too little princess' was one commentator's withering remark. Nevertheless, it set a benchmark for flamboyantly expensive 'fairy-tale' weddings and started a craze for gowns of meringue-like proportions.

Princess Diana was a perfect heroine for the yuppie decade. She had grown up with ponies and dancing lessons, lived in Chelsea and left her job as a nursery school teacher when she became engaged to the Prince of Wales. Before her wedding, her style was defined by pie-frill-collared blouses, Laura Ashley floral prints, country tweeds and the ubiquitous strand of pearls. After her two sons were born, she was transformed into a svelte sophisticate and her every movement was documented. She hung out with rock stars, danced with John Travolta at the White House, and wore designer fashion for every public appearance. Before the decade was out she had transformed from 'Shy Di' into '*Dynasty* Di', thanks to the statement-shouldered evening gowns and ladylike suits she favoured from British designers such as Catherine Walker, Victor Edelstein and Bruce Oldfield.

The 'early' Princess of Wales, during a trip to Australia in 1983. Here she wears a sprigged, romantic creation by Jan van Velden. As the decade progressed, she would be seen in increasingly more daring styles.

REI KAWAKUBO

Catwalk radical

Arriving in Paris in 1981, the ridicule and rejection that greeted Rei Kawakubo (1942–) was in inverse proportion to the respect she is afforded today. Her 1982 show, whose aesthetic flew in the face of European sensibilities, was denounced as 'post-apocalyptic'. The fashion press were stunned and delighted in equal measure.

Kawakubo was widely misunderstood. What appeared to be a mission to destroy the codes of Western clothing was, in fact, quite the opposite: Kawakubo set out to analyse and scrutinize the components of fashion, deconstructing them before reconstructing them in more interesting and exciting ways. Her avant-garde approach was influenced by the Japanese tradition of wabi-sabi, a philosophy derived from Zen Buddhism that finds beauty in imperfection and impermanence.

Kawakubo was all about change. For her, modern women no longer needed to submit to men, and the designer had a vision of how they could assert themselves – 'Comme des Garçons'. Out went the geisha of the Japan of her childhood, as did the sexily dressed Western doll. In came the new woman who did not seek to please, who defined her personality and power with clothes that were not for bimbos.

With her unsmiling face, her geometric bob and unyielding authorititiveness, Rei Kawakubo embodied this new woman. She garnered an immediate and dedicated following among artists and intellectuals, who appreciated the loosely cut clothes made from rare materials imported from Japan.

Rei Kawakubo at the opening of her Comme des Garçons shop in New York City's Henri Bendel store in 1983. The designer's deliberately unfinished clothes excited many who were questioning the definition of luxury.

COMME des GARÇONS

WHAM!
Pastel popstrels

The combination of George Michael's (1963–) leonine blond locks and perfect teeth and Andrew Ridgeley's (1963–) smouldering stare, their perma-tans, bony ankles and bare chests under bomber jackets, the perky lyrics and aerobic choreography, perfectly summed up the frivolity of the decade.

For the debut performance of 'Young Guns (Go for It!)' on the BBC's *Top of the Pops*, George Michael wore espadrilles, a suede jacket with rolled-up sleeves and jeans with rolled-up hems. The boys from Bushey were an overnight pop sensation – heart-throbs with headlining hair and a catchy tune. By the end of 1983, Wham! was shouldering up to Duran Duran and Culture Club in the big league of British pop. Requisite notoriety with its attendant column inches was duly achieved when they were reported to have padded out their shorts with shuttlecocks on their Club Fantastic Tour.

Ridgeley was the stylist. It was he who was responsible for the dizzying wardrobe that spanned unlikely extremes, from the black leather-clad bad boys of 'Bad Boys' (1983) to the pastel popstrels of 'Wake Me Up Before You Go-Go' (1984). It is still one of the great mysteries of the industry how Ridgeley persuaded George Michael to pitch up at the Brit Awards wearing a suit that made him look like Colonel Sanders.

Wham! on the Channel 4 TV music show *The Tube*. George Michael now looks back and admits he and band mate Ridgeley could have styled themselves better. 'I didn't use a stylist. I don't think I could have afforded one,' he says.

ANNIE LENNOX

She-man chic

In a decade of iconoclasts who recognized and revelled in the revolutionary power of the three-minute pop video, Annie Lennox (1954–) managed to be a game changer. In the rising tide of rebels, she rose above the rest. She was 'the white Grace Jones', a style icon for the androgynous fashion outbreak of the 1980s – a style choice that provoked virulent speculation about her sexuality and even her status as a female.

With neither feminine nor masculine looks, her sharp tailoring and gender-bending performances in videos such as 'Who's That Girl' (1983), Lennox was so effective at confounding preconceptions that for years people thought she was gay. Lennox's presentation of her inner masculinity sparked endless controversy. Novelist Anne Rice wrote that she 'coolly jumbled all our safe ideas about gender'.

For Lennox, though, it was more about dressing up and image than sexual politics. She grew up in Aberdeen: 'A city so grey, I'd spend all my time in the art gallery because it was the only beautiful place to be. I was obsessed with bright, shiny things …' After the first Eurythmics album *Into the Garden* in 1981, she quickly tired of being called 'the British Blondie', and the peroxide was replaced with a carrot-topped crew cut and mannish suits – the stark, transgressive look she donned for the 'Sweet Dreams' video in 1983.

Annie Lennox's distinctive image criss-crossed gender boundaries and brought a forthright sexuality to the world of the female singer-songwriter.

BODYMAP
London's dream team

In the 1980s the global fashion talent spotters once again turned to London for inspiration – thanks, for the most part, to a thriving music, street fashion and club scene. By 1982 a fledgling London Fashion Week was jostling for position on the international calendar, and the sensational arrivistes of the year were Stevie Stewart and David Holah (both 1958–), graduates from Middlesex Polytechnic who together had formed Bodymap.

Stalwarts of the Blitz Club with a following of art college acolytes, contemporary dancers, performance artists and pop stars, Stewart and Holah redefined the catwalk show. While even the wildest shows in Paris were still pretty conventional, opening with daywear and closing with the bride, Bodymap's presentations by comparison were a veritable romp. Their surreal titles hinted at the mayhem: 'Barbie Takes a Trip around Nature's Cosmic Curves', 'Querelle Meets Olive Oil' and 'The Cat in the Hat Takes a Rumble with the Techno Fish'. These were never going to be understated affairs.

The duo could always be relied upon to rally famous friends to make cameo catwalk appearances. Boy George was known to take a turn. The dancer Michael Clark and the artists Trojan and Leigh Bowery were regular enough to be considered part of the Bodymap 'family'. And long before Benetton's controversial advertising campaigns, Stevie Stewart and David Holah used models of all sizes and ages (including their mothers) in a show called 'Family'.

In spite of adding affordable collections of swimwear and hosiery and a second line called B-Basic, aimed at expanding their youthful clientele, the pair's incandescent success fizzled out in the face of economic downturn in 1986.

Influenced by the distorted silhouettes of the Japanese avant-garde, Bodymap's sinuous jerseys and knits, along with textile designer Hilde Smith's prints, shaped a vision that was totally innovative in its hedonistic, youthful energy.

JEAN PAUL GAULTIER

Paris's eternal enfant terrible

Paris 1981: François Mitterrand became president of a country in crisis. People took to the streets to express dissatisfaction with economic stagnation and rising unemployment. Minorities, including gay men, demonstrated to assert their rights. It was in the context of this social change and unrest that Jean Paul Gaultier (1952–) became France's rising fashion star. In his own humble words, in a television interview at the time, his look was simply 'classical basics thrown together in a paradoxical fashion'. Dubbed the *enfant terrible* of the catwalk, Gaultier embodied the rebellious energy that was forcing change in a change-averse France.

Witty irreverence as well as sexual ambivalence became a hallmark of his style. His Autumn/Winter 1984/85 show recast the corset as outerwear, with an exaggerated conical-breasted silhouette. For Spring/Summer 1985 he explored the theme of androgyny, putting men in skirts – an updated version of the kilt that would become an enduring motif in his collections. His work was a style salvo aimed at destroying the traditional masculine and feminine wardrobe and all the social snobbery and conventions that went with it.

Gaultier broke down levels of good taste and embraced 'low' culture. He presented men on stage as sex objects. He dabbled in ever-increasing extremes of exposure, cutting away everything but the structure, until dresses consisted of more exercise-toned body than cloth. He dressed male models in gingham and open-toed, high-heeled sneakers. He dressed Madonna in crucifixes and sex-shop corsetry and produced the cone bra for her 1990 Blonde Ambition tour.

Right: Jean Paul Gaultier poses with friends outside a Paris Métro station in 1985, wearing some of his ready-to-wear creations. Below: Gaultier sports a suit of his own creation, 1984.

KATHARINE HAMNETT
Catwalk campaigner

In 1984 Katharine Hamnett (1947–) provided one of the defining fashion moments of the decade when she greeted Prime Minister Mrs Thatcher at a government reception wearing one of her T-shirts emblazoned with the slogan '58% DON'T WANT PERSHING'. Her inspiration was the anti-nuclear women's protests at Greenham Common airbase in England where she herself 'manned' the barricades.

Hamnett founded her own label in 1979 and became one of the most copied designers in the world. Her show was one of the greatest draws at London Fashion Week, pulling in audiences of press and buyers from around the globe. Her clothes were based on workwear: simple, utilitarian shapes in serviceable and comfortable cotton drill or billowy parachute silk. She managed to become something of a rarity in British fashion at the time: a global commercial success.

Slogan T-shirts became part of her collection in 1983 and were massively successful after they became standard issue for image-conscious pop bands. Andrew Ridgeley and George Michael wore the 'CHOOSE LIFE' slogan T-shirt for their 'Wake Me Up Before You Go Go' video. Hamnett later commented: 'Fashion gets so much publicity that it's almost disgusting. So I thought I'd put this to good use and send some political, social messages out there on T-shirts: messages people need to be aware of, which might make them think, talk to each other and maybe even generate some action …'

Fashion confronts the establishment in the famous handshake between Hamnett and Mrs Thatcher in 1984. During the 1980s, fashion went political in a way it had never done before.

MADONNA
Made on MTV

Madonna (1958–) burst into our lives in 1984 and for the ensuing quarter of a century rarely left our screens.

Crucifixes, fingerless gloves and ratty hair tied up in floppy bows were the instantly recognizable elements that added up to the 'bad girl' look she wore in Susan Seidelman's 1985 movie *Desperately Seeking Susan*. It was a thrift-store mash-up that inspired wannabes in shopping malls and on high-street corners across the globe.

Beyond that explosive debut, it was Madonna Ciccone's knack for reinvention, in the age of a nascent MTV, that really propelled her career. Her ability to serve herself up serially as dramatically different personae cast her as a direct descendant of David Bowie (in the costume department at least). Whether in her Gaultier conical bras or any number of religious incarnations, Madonna's chameleon sense of style has never failed to keep the fashion world on its toes. The trashy punk dressed in lace and denim in *Desperately Seeking Susan* was soon ditched for a glamorous Marilyn Monroe avatar for 'Material Girl', which in turn would be discarded for the provocative Gaultier-dressed dominatrix of the early 1990s.

Arguably, her risqué style opened the door for a more individualistic trend in mainstream teenage fashion. But Madonna's wardrobe not only created a signature '80s look, it also helped pioneer an empowered attitude among young women of not only that decade but beyond.

Madonna with DJ Jellybean Benitez at the opening of the Manhattan club Private Eyes. Madonna's first incarnation married thrift style with high-end labels.

Giorgio Armani (see page 28) enjoyed a huge windfall of publicity for something he had nothing to do with. The rumpled linen jackets worn, with sleeves rolled up, by Don Johnson and Philip Michael Thomas in the hit 1980s TV series *Miami Vice*, were widely credited to the Italian designer. The show attracted millions of viewers, who tuned in regularly just to check out the clothes. And retailers, worldwide, cashed in on the *Miami Vice* style of unconstructed blazers and pleated trousers.

The show's costume designer, Bambi Breakstone, defined the detectives' cover-boy style, drawing on the work of designers such as Hugo Boss and Gianni Versace, though it was Nino Cerruti who had created the original look. Breakstone admitted she had been briefed to be unashamedly fashion forward: 'The concept of the show was to be on top of all the latest fashion trends in Europe.'

The show drew heavily on 1980s culture and music. The producers would dedicate a significant budget per episode to buy the rights to original recordings, and promoters soon noticed that getting a song played on *Miami Vice* was a reliable way to boost record sales. But it is Italian men's fashion that owes most to the series. From Don Johnson's daily uniform of unstructured blazer, T-shirt, white linen pants and slip-on loafers (worn without socks) to the duo's designer stubble and sunglasses, the cops' wardrobe became a defining menswear look of the 1980s.

The Italian-inspired costume design of *Miami Vice* inspired a generation of Armani-wearing urban peacocks, for whom rolled-up jacket sleeves, loafers and designer stubble were the ultimate style statements.

MICHAEL JACKSON

King of pop

The glove, the sequins, the regalia, the military jacket, the loafers, white socks and aviator shades: Michael Jackson (1958–2009) created an image in the 1980s that confirmed his status as 'King of Pop' for a generation of adoring subjects. Decades later, the look still resonates, both on the street and on international catwalks. From Balmain to Isabel Marant, from Chanel to Givenchy, there has barely been a design house that has not bumped into the style *oeuvre* of Michael Jackson at some stage over the decades between the release of *Thriller* (1982) and his death in 2009.

For 25 years, Michael Bush and Dennis Tompkins were the designers behind many of Jackson's tour costumes and personal wardrobe. They designed tens of thousands of pieces, working from a Michael mannequin in their studio that replicated the singer's exact measurements. Michael Bush recalls: 'Michael loved military style, Egyptian styles and the image of royalty as you can see in many of his most famous costumes and personal outfits. When we designed, we designed for showtime, no matter what the occasion.'

Accessories were key to Jackson's look. He embraced chunky belts, armbands, sequins, hats, straps, ties, patches and sunglasses. He gave pieces as simple as military badges, the fedora and white socks an imprint that, for a time, was as powerful as his music. But the most iconic Jackson accessory remains the legendary single white glove. No matter what Jackson wore, before or after he introduced the white glove to his aesthetic in the 1980s, it would be the defining fashion moment in a career full of memorable fashion moments.

Showtime! Jackson never essayed understatement. His glorious outfits were a fabulous '80s mash-up of Las Vegas and West Point, carnival and military parade.

PRINCE
New rock royalty

Throughout the 1980s Prince (1958–) ploughed a singularly unique style furrow. The purveyor of sexually charged pop songs, with his powerhouse, multiethnic, feminized persona, he confounded audiences and critics alike. His stage presence might have seemed yet another example of strutting Latin machismo, but at the same time he was a mascaraed fashion plate, androgynous in chiffon ruffles. Prince was shocking and confusing in generously equal measures.

From 1978, the year his first album, *For You*, came out, to 1982, just before the release of *1999*, he rocked a disparate combination of fashion elements. It was a look that took the world, let alone his native Minneapolis, by surprise. While he could handle a guitar like a rock virtuoso, his wardrobe was a world away from the Springsteen leather jacket and raggedy jeans. His typical stage wardrobe consisted of skimpy shorts, Speedo trunks, skin-tight thigh-high socks, and vertiginous heels, despite all of which he could still leap from a grand piano and land in the splits. His bare chest was only occasionally covered by a coat.

In the context of American rock, Prince's preoccupation with gender-bending was startling. He went for bright eye makeup and dressed like a rococo street urchin. In 1983 he accepted an award from a Minneapolis weekly newspaper for Minnesota Musician of the Year, wearing a black trench coat and white go-go boots. He has even been known to perform in nothing but boots and a pair of bikini underpants.

Prince on stage in the mid-1980s. *Rolling Stone* noted: 'Prince does not dress like your average rock star.' His diminutive stature and rococo stylings subverted the usual clichés of male rock 'n' roll culture.

SADE

Siren of understatement

In the 1980s it was pretty difficult to get ahead in the music business without a look, and what a look Sade (1959–) had – the hair scraped back off a high forehead, hooped earrings, scarlet mouth and a dancer's body dressed in a backless black cocktail dress. She was instantly memorable.

Born Helen Folasade Adu in Nigeria, Sade studied fashion at Saint Martins College of Art when she moved to London at age 18. She started her own menswear line and her career course, it seemed, was set. Her singing voice was discovered when she obliged a friend with a favour and stood in to do some backing vocals. 'When singing came up, I didn't think about making a career of it,' Sade told *Rolling Stone*. 'I thought, I don't do crocheting and I don't play badminton. This could be a good hobby!' The success of her first single put paid to any ambitions she may have had to launch a menswear empire.

'Your Love Is King' was released in early 1984 and charted at number 6 in the UK. The song's video cemented Sade's status as a style star. She was featured on the cover of *The Face* that same year, and magazines from *Vogue* to *Elle* fought over the few interviews she agreed to give. Her debut album, *Diamond Life*, sold more than four million around the world. In an industry of limelight-hogging showmen, Sade was the queen of cool understatement. She had an elegance based on absolute simplicity, her smooth, husky voice and her penchant for siren dresses and mannish suits recalling the great New York jazz clubs of the 1930s and '40s.

Sade's pared-back style was for many a breath of fresh air in the overheated atmosphere of 1980s pop.

THIERRY MUGLER
Catwalk impresario

In the 1980s Thierry Mugler (1948–) became a formidable force on the French fashion stage. With the support of Melka Tréanton, fashion editor at French *Elle*, he had been building his own business throughout the 1970s. By 1978 he was ready to open his own shop on Paris's place des Victoires. Defying the luxury tradition, he went straight into ready-to-wear, resisting the call of couture. He also opened his own factory in Angers – he was the only European designer to make such an investment and it helped to establish him, not only as a creative visionary, but also as a successful entrepreneur.

Mugler changed the way fashion collections were presented, too. His shows took place, not in salons with little gilded chairs, but in vast tents and with dramatic staging. They were 'happenings' that attracted the press, buyers and hangers-on in numbers that rivalled rock concerts. 'Theatre is everything,' the designer once declared. 'My life is a stage.'

Mugler also insisted that 'a well-constructed body needs shoulders'. In this, the Mugler woman was never disappointed. She got those shoulders and much more besides: a hand-span waist, a plunging neckline and an air of haughty froideur that was perfectly in tune with the narcissism of the decade.

Mugler led the field in a return to an engineered, highly structured look – a Mugler suit was like the bodywork of a car, often complete with accessories such as handcrafted fins and hardware. In pursuit of his idealized futuristic power-babe, for two decades he called upon his Angers factory to deliver ever more extraordinary feats of fashion production.

Baroque splendour: a 'typical' Mugler creation, from his Autumn/Winter 1984–85 collection. Gold, with its connotations of fabulous wealth and space-age glamour, was an enduring leitmotif.

AZZEDINE ALAÏA

A unique body of work

A student of sculpture at the Ecole des Beaux-Arts in Tunis, Azzedine Alaïa (1940–) was to become the most Parisian of all couturiers. He arrived in Paris in 1957 and started as he has continued, making his way *hors de l'établissement*. He managed a lightning five-day stint at Dior and a couple of seasons at Guy Laroche before abandoning the gilded couture salons to set up on his own to dress private clients.

Alaïa fits one of his contour-hugging dresses to pop chanteuse Grace Jones. Alaïa's genius was to marry understated classicism with an avant-garde vibe.

The press were quick to spot him. *Elle* featured a coat he designed for Les Fourrures de la Madeleine in 1979, and a leather piece with a constellation of rivets was shot for the style magazine *Dépêche Mode* in 1980. Emboldened, Alaïa showed his first collection under his own name in 1981, in his small apartment in rue de Bellechasse, attracting a galaxy of stars that included Grace Jones and Tina Turner.

Alaïa created a new way for women to dress, but more by reinterpretation than reinvention. His work was radical, nonetheless. In a decade that celebrated style over substance, he dressed the female body without artifice, with no weapons other than skilful cutting and innovations such as seams that snaked around the body's contours with engineered precision. He created figure-hugging bodysuits and leggings that accentuated every curve while at the same time magically smoothing out imperfections.

But Alaïa remained a best-kept insider secret, mostly by the carousel of supermodels, artists and assorted intelligentsia who gathered nightly at his kitchen table (where he liked to cook dinner himself). In 1986 he was outed from the inner circle and established forever in the popular imagination through Robert Palmer's video 'Addicted to Love'. The singer's backing band was four Alaïa-clad women, their hair identically scraped back, lips identically scarlet and all in identical black-knit dresses.

THE BRAT PACK

Triumphing over the trials of youth

Diane Lane was the cinema sensation of 1982 when she starred as Cherry Valance alongside Matt Dillon, Tom Cruise, Patrick Swayze and Rob Lowe in Francis Ford Coppola's *The Outsiders*. In a reference to the hedonistic 'Rat Pack' of the 1950s led by Frank Sinatra and Dean Martin, Andy Warhol dubbed her 'the undisputed female lead of Hollywood's new Rat Pack'. Three years later, following the release of John Hughes's *The Breakfast Club* (1985; starring Molly Ringwald, Emilio Estevez and Ally Sheedy) and Joel Schumacher's *St. Elmo's Fire* (1985; with Rob Lowe), *New York Magazine*'s David Blum christened the new generation of young actors the 'Brat Pack'.

Molly Ringwald, Martha Plimpton, Demi Moore and Winona Ryder were the undisputed queens of the scene. But what was different about them was they weren't goddesses; nor were they sex kittens: they were just spirited adolescents with charisma overload. It was the era of the coming-of-age movie when disaffected youth took centre stage. Key fashion moments include Molly Ringwald's creative deconstruction of her hideous prom dress in *Pretty in Pink* (1986), Judd Nelson's fingerless gloves and shades in *The Breakfast Club,* and the dirty Converse trainers and plaid shirts, prefiguring grunge, in *St. Elmo's Fire*.

The Brat Pack channelled the teenage angst of white middle-class youth on the threshold of adulthood in an era of conformity. Their nod to rebellion was packaged in a style that was more flea market than high fashion. They mixed hand-me-downs and cast-offs: boyfriend blazers with rolled-up sleeves, T-shirts, denim plastered with badges, and ankle-length skirts. It was the supremacy of the DIY style.

The beginning of grunge? Movies such as *The Breakfast Club* popularized a déclassé style of denim, T-shirts and rolled-up sleeves. It was more yuppie than street, all the same.

THEY ONLY MET ONCE, BUT IT CHANGED THEIR LIVES FOREVER.

They were five total strangers, with nothing in common,
meeting for the first time.
A brain, a beauty, a jock, a rebel and a recluse.

Before the day was over, they broke the rules.
Bared their souls.
And touched each other in a way
they never dreamed possible.

THE BREAKFAST CLUB

A JOHN HUGHES Film · An A&M FILMS/CHANNEL Production "THE BREAKFAST CLUB"
Starring EMILIO ESTEVEZ · PAUL GLEASON · ANTHONY MICHAEL HALL · JUDD NELSON · MOLLY RINGWALD · ALLY SHEEDY
Written and Directed by JOHN HUGHES Edited by DEDE ALLEN A.C.E. Music Composed by KEITH FORSEY Co-Producer MICHELLE MANNING Executive Producers GIL FRIESEN and ANDREW MEYER
Produced by NED TANEN and JOHN HUGHES A UNIVERSAL PICTURE

N·S·S #850002

JANE FONDA

Fabulously fit

1985

Responsibility for the decade's obsession with the body beautiful can be laid squarely at the door of one woman: Jane Fonda (1937–). The movie star, political activist and Academy Award winner launched an entirely new (and very lucrative) career after injury on the set of *The China Syndrome* (1979) forced her to find an alternative to the ballet classes she took to keep in shape. She signed up for aerobics under the supervision of Leni Cazden, whose method evolved into the Jane Fonda Workout.

Technology helped Fonda reinvent herself as a fitness guru. Her first exercise video was released in 1982 and the uptake among owners of VCRs, then the cutting edge in home entertainment gadgetry, achieved sales topping a million. Over the next twelve years, 5 books, 23 videos and 13 audio tapes helped millions of women pursue Fonda's quest for 'the burn'. She explained: 'In order to have an effect, I would have to work out hard enough so that I could feel the sensation that I would describe as a burn. Go for the burn, go until you can feel that thing, and then you know it's going to make a difference.'

'Feel the burn' became a Fonda catchphrase, and a fitness craze swept Europe and America. The fashionable preoccupations of the decade became health, beauty, youthfulness and sex appeal. Accordingly, the diet, health-club and fitness equipment industries boomed. Biker shorts, headbands, sweatshirts and legwarmers became streetwear, and Lycra was transformed from a fibre known mostly to lingerie and hosiery manufacturers into a global mega-brand for its developer and manufacturer, DuPont.

Jane Fonda launched not just a fitness revolution but a streetwear revolution, too.

RAY PETRI : BUFFALO

The stylist's stylist

London in the 1980s was a melting pot of pop culture, politics and the rediscovered power of branded products. Ray Petri (1948–89) was the city's most articulate interpreter of the *zeitgeist*. Founder of Buffalo (a creative collective, a style manifesto, an attitude), he was the stylist's stylist, and one of the first. His work for *The Face*, *Arena* and *iD* is still hauntingly powerful.

Petri couldn't find any models he liked at the established agencies. They specialized in the commercial look of the day, which was almost exclusively white, so he went out on the street. Petri is most often remembered for discovering Nick Kamen, who stripped off his Levi's in a launderette and made 501s the must-have of the decade. It was one of the most iconic images of the 1980s, but it happened largely because Ray Petri had managed to break the mould of accepted beauty. 'The models had to have the right spirit. The look wasn't enough. It had to go deeper. They had to be humble but proud at the same time,' remembers Buffalo collaborator Mitzi Lorenz.

Buffalo is mostly remembered for its boys. But it made stars of women, too. Talisa Soto was the only internationally established fashion model in the group, and her relationship with Nick Kamen was at the heart of the Buffalo family. Among the striking similarities they shared was their androgynous beauty: his with a delicacy that was almost feminine; hers with a toughness that was singularly male. They appeared together on a 1985 cover of *The Face*. 'Somewhere between Nick and Talisa was Ray's ideal,' says Nick's brother, Barry Kamen. 'The couple summed up what Buffalo was about. She was a tough Hispanic American from the Bronx and Nick was an English half-Burmese boy from Essex.'

Images from the Buffalo collective: the model Lindsey Thurlow (right) photographed by Jamie Morgan for *The Face,* and the pop singer Neneh Cherry, at the start of her career. Buffalo celebrated the extraordinary in the ordinary.

HIP-HOP
Rapping radicals

The years between the commercial breakthrough of Run-D.M.C. and the arrival of gangsta rap with NWA in the late 1980s are considered by aficionados to be hip-hop's golden years. In terms of fashion, Run-D.M.C. is credited with defining the identity of hip-hop, drawing a line under the disco dressing of Grand Master Flash. Hip-hop came from the street, first as backing music for the local block party but then, as rap pioneer Chuck D put it, as 'The Black CNN', with lyrics commenting on social issues and reporting on conditions in the lives of those traditionally shunted to the edges of mainstream America.

Run-D.M.C's look was an expression of black power. They wouldn't be caught rapping in high-fashion labels. They stuck to their street clothes and to the brands their community was wearing: Adidas and Kangol. Typically, hip-hop artists wore tracksuits, bomber jackets, large glasses, Kangol bucket hats and Adidas Superstar shell-toe sneakers with oversized laces. Or they wore no laces at all, taking their inspiration from prison inmates whose laces were always confiscated.

Heavy gold jewellery was power play – a signifier of wealth and success. The guys wore heavy gold chains; the female equivalent was door-knocker earrings, as seen on female artists Salt-N-Pepa. For all its concern with street cred, hip-hop was not immune to the lure of luxury and, like the yuppies of the 1980s in their designer labels, the rappers gradually began to display their wealth through status symbols. Hundred-dollar sneakers and designer tracksuits were accessorized with blatant badges of wealth such as the emblems of luxury cars.

The cover of Run–D.M.C.'s single 'Walk This Way' (1986). The group members sport the 'classic' hip-hop look: bomber jackets, jeans and white sneakers.

SOCIAL CONSCIENCE

The good deed decade

The 1980s are often dismissed as one of narcissistic hedonism, yet the decade also saw a surge in political awareness and heightened social activism. The face of fundraising changed for ever. Where once there were old ladies rattling tins in the shopping centre on a Saturday, funds and awareness were raised, 1980s style, through the consciences of pop stars, fashion designers and celebrities. Mass charity events such as Live Aid raised money for famine in Ethiopia, while in 1985 five thousand people gathered inside London's Albert Hall under the banner of Fashion Aid – 'for an evening of spectacle and glamour' … and fundraising.

Animal rights activism also got a makeover. Lynx was one of the most successful pressure groups of the 1980s. The charity, which boasted the support of celebrities including Neil Kinnock and Elton John, shot to prominence with a controversial advertising campaign. Shot by David Bailey, it featured a model trailing blood from a full-length fur coat. The caption read: 'It took 13 dumb animals to make this and only one to wear it.' In 1986 Liz Tilberis banned the running of fur features in *Vogue*.

The greatest challenge of all, however, was faced when HIV/AIDS decimated the fashion industry and inspired activism in an industry not naturally given to selfless acts of generosity. Few, eventually, would be left untouched or unaffected by the virus's terrifying spread.

Celebrities at 1985's Fashion Aid: Paula Yates (right) and Freddie Mercury and Jane Seymour (below). Eighties fashion, for all its frivolity, was characterized by a new political engagement.

BOY GEORGE

Peacock of pop

1987

Fashion's fascination with the peacock parade that defined street and clubland style fuelled a very 1980s renaissance of the phenomenon of the cross-dressing pop star. Men were dressing, if not to look like women, then at least as sexual ciphers. And, on the flipside, women dressed to look like men. Alternatively, both sexes met mid-way to look neither male nor female, but some exotic assexual creature located between the two.

In the early 1980s Boy George (born George Alan O'Dowd in 1961) blazed a trail for the gender-bender style. The singer Marilyn followed, but, in an effort to become a more serious performer, George dropped the frock and quickly fell into the fickle '80s fashion abyss. Around the time of Boy George's rise, Annie Lennox, too, essayed cross-dressing, appearing in the video for 'Sweet Dreams' sporting a short orange haircut and mannish suit.

While his band, Culture Club, donned American baseball gear, with sweatshirts and huge padded shoulders, Boy George swiftly moved on from a large Stars-and-Stripes coat worn with an oversize straw top hat to his 'Egyptian headdress' look. He had his clothes made by Dexter Wong, who operated out of the Hyper Hyper emporium on London's Kensington High Street, and accessorized them with bold Monty Don necklaces.

Boy George's distinctive style was part showmanship, part radical statement, in a decade that subverted gender stereotypes and saw the first great commercial flowering of modern gay culture.

CLAUDE MONTANA

Drama king

In the 1980s Claude Montana (1949–) was *the* go-to designer for melodramatic glamour. His lofty, architectural style totally dispensed with any romantic vestiges of the 1970s bohemian hippy, but he was also diametrically opposed to the sombre cerebral style of Kawakubo and Yamamoto. His clothes were all about Gallic sex appeal, hauteur and colour. He presented women with the armour he believed they wanted. The classic Montana silhouette was an inverted triangle with large shoulders and a tiny waist, and generally involved a liberal helping of glossy black leather. His high-vamp, high-price chic flaunted the sexual marketability of women.

Fashion fans flocked to see and be seen at Montana's catwalk extravaganzas. Wicked, aloof, glacial, bondaged, his catwalk queens stalked the runway with girded loins, tight skirts, aggressive shoulders, and revealing corsetry worn like armour plating. His love of leather coats and capes got him shot down more than once for their alleged Nazi references. Nevertheless, his shows were colossal publicity magnets and, even in the chicest and most strait-laced boutiques, his look was a commercial winner. Even his fiercest critics had to admit he had his finger on a sociological pulse.

Montana invented the 'total look'. Montana pieces did not slip easily in and out of an eclectic wardrobe – people bought the entire Montana range. The 'look' filtered to the high street at cheaper prices, spawning a younger generation of sharp-shouldered sirens who brooked no nonsense.

Montana takes the applause at his Spring/Summer 1988 collection. Montana's heavily structured, fetishized style may not have been exactly 'politically correct', but it nonetheless caught the *zeitgeist*.

KARL LAGERFELD AT CHANEL
Fashioning a French icon

In 1983 Karl Lagerfeld (1933–) became chief designer of the Chanel couture house. He already had a reputation as a prolific designer: since the 1970s he had designed collections for Chloé in Paris and Fendi in Rome, stopping off at MaxMara in Milan along the way, while also taking the time to develop collections in his own name. Chanel, meanwhile, was a faded brand, although with the singular advantage that, unlike so many of its rivals and contemporaries, it had never sold its assets to licensees. But it had nothing much to offer beyond some dowdy tweed suits.

Thanks to the ingenious Lagerfeld and the company's careful handling of its branded perfume and accessories, within a decade Chanel was a $1 billion company. Lagerfeld was an inveterate modernizer, considering himself an outsider to the French fashion establishment, which he loathed for its conservatism. He had spent years minutely studying the legacy of Coco Chanel and now set about reinventing it. A natural communicator, Lagerfeld could host press conferences in five languages and had an instinctive understanding of the power of the media. He had an equal understanding of what women wanted.

His collections for Chanel almost parodied the new status dressing, shamelessly exploiting the 'double C' logo and classic leitmotifs such as the camellia brooch and the diamond quilting. Nevertheless, the clientele took it seriously, sporting quilted leather handbags, large gilt CC earrings and miniskirts hung with chains on fashionable streets everywhere. Lagerfeld's appeal to the newly moneyed was a significant engine of Chanel's resurgent success.

Lagerfeld reinvented Chanel for the 1980s, trading on the brand's famous trappings to create a signature style for the ultra-rich, here modelled by Inès de la Fressange.

JASPER CONRAN

Embracing the business of British fashion

Though the international press may have focused on London as the provider of wacky amateurism, the city did have a hard core of professional designers. In the 1980s the ranks of Jean Muir and Zandra Rhodes were joined by Sheridan Barnett, Alistair Blair and Jasper Conran (1959–), who managed, in a world of flamboyant showmen, to combine creativity with business acumen. Back then, British fashion typically aspired to be art: fashion shows were 'happenings' and the clothes often came a poor second to the cult of the designer. Fashion entrepreneurialism was a gutsy position to take when the industry equated 'selling' with 'selling out'.

The son of Sir Terence Conran, Britain's best-known designer, Jasper was accepted at the Parsons School of Design in New York at the age of sixteen. There he caught the tail end of Manhattan hedonism, becoming a Studio 54 habitué while still in his teens. He witnessed, too, the rise of a new generation of American designers, Donna Karan, Calvin Klein and Michael Kors among them, who responded to the wardrobe needs of the modern woman in the most practical ways. In 1979, aged just nineteen, he designed his first womenswear collection under his own name, and the following year he was invited to show as part of the London Designer collections.

His New York experience shaped both his attitude to fashion and his strong commercial sense. American fashion appealed to what Conran calls his 'sensible approach'. He quickly learned to accept that sensible clothes didn't always make the headlines, but it was an attitude that did not hold him back. While other British designers enjoyed meteoric rises and dramatic falls, over the years he built up a faithful clientele who loved his quietly confident clothes – not least Princess Diana, who often relied on Conran to dress her for public appearances.

Jasper Conran with Bianca Jagger in 1987. Conran brought a badly needed dose of sense and sensibility to British fashion of the 1980s.

CHRISTIAN LACROIX

Delightfully *de trop*

In 1982 Christian Lacroix (1951–) exploded onto the fashion scene as the couturier at the forgotten Parisian house of Patou. With the economic boom, luxury was back in style for the first time in years. And with it came a market for clothes in which the newly wealthy could dress up and show off.

The designers of the futuristic avant-garde may have been darlings of the fashion press, but Lacroix still captured imaginations with his diametrically opposed fashion language centred on the bustles, bows, corsets and crinolines found in eighteenth-century rococo artists like Boucher and Fragonard. He conjured a colourful, riotous fashion vision, mixing the ruffles and feathers of Toulouse-Lautrec's cancan dancers with lace and prints inspired by the gypsies of his native Provence.

The intricacies of his embroideries and passementeries, and the work in feathers and flowers focused renewed attention on the skills of the artisans of the couture ateliers, who had fallen out of favour with modern designers who followed a less decorative and more utilitarian path. Through Lacroix's collections, their work once again inspired the audiences with wonder. 'Personally I've always hovered between the purity of structures and the ecstasy of ornament,' said the designer who always faced down the minimalists with a style that was defiantly *de trop*.

Christian Lacroix with Jane Seymour in 1987. Lacroix's puffball skirt – a balloon of taffeta or satin – would become the *fin-de-siècle* ball gown. A short version teamed with bullfighter's jacket, worn with sheer stockings and towering heels, ensured that legs became the decade's favourite erogenous zone.

WHITNEY HOUSTON

Pop's most glamorous girl next door

Whitney Houston (1963–2012) started working as a fashion model after a photographer saw her at Carnegie Hall singing with her mother, Cissy Houston. She worked for *Cosmopolitan* and *Glamour* and became one of the first black models to feature on the cover of *Seventeen* magazine. By the time she launched her career as a singer, she was already one of the most sought-after teen models of the time.

In the context of the gender-benders, bad boy rockers and pop vixens of the 1980s Billboard charts, Whitney Houston was seen as a 'good girl' with a squeaky-clean image. Compared to Madonna or Annie Lennox, she was not a fashion trailblazer, but her sorority style and peerless voice made her an inspiration for millions of young women. In the landscape of the 1980s it took guts to be the iconic girl next door.

Houston's styling choices were undoubtedly tame. She bounced around the stage dressed in sneakers, stonewashed jeans, box-fresh white T-shirts and modestly large gold hoop earrings. She wore a sweatshirt and tied her hair in a stretchy bandanna to sing the 'Star-spangled Banner' for the opening of the Superbowl, looking more like she was on her way to a workout than the opening of America's largest televised sporting event. Her dressed-up options were scarcely more adventurous, often featuring spangled black or white stretch dresses. She had a penchant for wide-shouldered suits and white cloche hats.

In a world where stars universally aspired to radical, subversive images, Whitney Houston was the approachable diva.

The exception proves the rule: Houston's dress sense was usually determinedly girl-next-door, but would occasionally veer into wilder territory, as in this image from her 1987 video for 'I Want to Dance with Somebody'.

YOHJI YAMAMOTO
Catwalk minimalist

When the Japanese arrived in Paris in the 1980s, their pauper style was diametrically opposed to the theatrical modernism of Claude Montana (see page 78) and Thierry Mugler (see page 62). They were distinctly cerebral and more sombre than the hedonistic French. Yohji Yamamoto (1943–) was arguably *anti-*fashion. 'I don't follow the trend,' he asserted. 'I don't chase the trend.' Together with his partner of the time, Rei Kawakubo of Comme des Garçons (see page 40), he rocked the fashion world. The effect was cataclysmic, 'like a nuclear explosion or a natural catastrophe,' said *Le Figaro*. The models had a robotic way of walking, wore no make up, had messy hair. There were no high heels, no sequins. Clothes had holes, were worn with clumpy shoes and had unfinished edges.

Yamamoto launched his first attack on that bastion of male respectability, the suit, breaking down its traditional appeal as a cloak of respectability. For women, he engineered a striking encounter between austere tailoring and pretty, loose-fitting softness. In his hands, black was revered as a true colour with depth and warmth; the simplicity of the white shirt was its luminous counterpoint.

The spirit of Japanese dress has always remained the foundation of Yamamoto's style. His clothing incorporates a fluid fullness and often conceals the body to increase its mystery. Unlike the super-heroes who stalked the runways of Mugler and Montana or the baroque flamboyance of a Christian Lacroix collection, Yamamoto took his inspiration from real people and the way they lived and thought.

Yamamoto's designs were guided by the sensuality of the fabric, until finally the shape of the garment emerged. Structure was combined with yielding fluidity as seen in this iconic photo by Nick Knight, one of the decades key style influencers.

MANOLO BLAHNIK

Superlative shoes

Manolo Blahnik's (1942–) background goes some way to explaining his aesthetic breadth. Born in the Canary Islands, his father was Czech and his mother Spanish. He studied literature and art at the University of Geneva before moving to Paris in 1968 to study art at the Ecole du Louvre. An encounter with the celebrated columnist and editor Diana Vreeland in New York City set him on his path as a shoe designer.

Blahnik moved to London in 1970 and, after designing shoes for Ossie Clark, launched his own label in 1973. However, in the beginning he resisted calling himself a designer, finding the description pretentious. He said simply: 'I deal in shoes.' It was not until 1978 that he began to take his business seriously. His ascent to fashion stardom was meteoric. In 1980 the *New York Times* voted him the most influential shoe designer in the world, and his tiny shop in Chelsea became a mecca for celebrities, socialites and the *jeunesse dorée* alike.

In the 1980s Blahnik cemented a reputation for elegance and the dizzying height of his heels. He had a singular talent for creating harmonious combinations of materials and an ability to move effortlessly from purest classicism to dazzling strokes of boldness. Women adored his work for its extreme femininity and provocative sexiness. A Blahnik shoe was a concoction of rococo lightness, extrovert élan and worldly sophistication. No wonder so many of them were displayed on their owners' mantelpieces as mini works of art when not being worn.

Manolo Blahnik surveys his creations in his London salon. Blahnik continued the grand tradition of elegant women's footwear through the gaudy faux pas of the 1970s and '80s.

PAUL SMITH

Rethinking British menswear

Sir Paul Smith (1946–) was the accidental fashion designer who completely overhauled and revived the British male wardrobe in the 1980s. He is almost single-handedly responsible for the rediscovery of traditional British tailoring, simultaneously refreshing it with flourishes of his characteristic eccentricity and humour.

In 1964 Paul Smith was a cyclist with his heart set on professional status. An accident put paid to that ambition, and when he got out of hospital he took up with a group of art students in his native Nottingham, who introduced him to the world of contemporary art and music. Encouraged by Pauline Denyer, whom he would later marry, he took evening classes in tailoring. He showed his first own-label menswear collection in Paris in 1976.

In 1979 Smith opened a boutique in Covent Garden's Floral Street, launching the area as the epicentre of London's fashionable scene. They came in droves for his idiosyncratic mixture of Oxbridge dandy meets gap-year surfer; chairman of the board meets high-school dropout. In the staple Paul Smith suit, the burgeoning tribes of media, advertising and music industry executives of the 1980s found their perfect sartorial expression – serious, but not too serious.

The success of his style lay somewhere on the fine line where, as he put it, 'Savile Row meets Mr Bean'. Smith's blend of classic British style combined with unabashedly bright colours conveyed a spirit that was offbeat to the point of eccentricity. By the end of the decade he had turned a quirky idea of Britishness into a globally recognized language.

Photographic portrait of Paul Smith, 1988. 'My thing has always been about maximizing Britishness,' he said in an interview in 1981. 'I don't like stupid ideas that can't be worn.'

WORKING GIRLS

Executive chic

In 1975 John Molloy published his book *Women Dress for Success*. Corporate America, followed quickly by Europe and Britain, took his ideas to heart and women traded their mismatched separates for a sober suit. Molloy's argument was based on the premise that 'the simple tailored wool suit in neutral navy or slate blue grey, worn with non-sexual blouses, imitated uniform of rank, which by design was authoritative.' He used exhaustive research to back up his theory that both clients and subordinates accepted the word of a female dressed in a suit with better grace than if she were wearing a fashion outfit. It was a theory that ran and ran: by the advent of the 1980s the entire Western corporate world was in thrall to the concept of power dressing.

During the decade the number of women in executive jobs was on the rise. Women jogged or worked out before going to the office, dealt with domestic crises on the phone and swapped their Stephane Kélian heels for sneakers in order to hurry home to play with the baby before transforming themselves into sex objects for a dinner out.

For the entire decade, fashion was obsessed with power dressing. The single most important element of power dressing was the shoulder pad, and barely a garment was constructed without them. In pursuit of an image that would convey assertiveness, affluence and success in the business and social world, large shoulder pads propped up everything from tailored jackets and cocktail dresses to pyjamas.

'I've got a head for business,' boasted Melanie Griffith in the movie *Working Girl* (1988), 'and a bod for sin.' By the late 1980s the female wool suit and 'non-sexual blouse' had taken on their own hard-edged glamour.

RIFAT OZBEK

Ottoman romance

Born in Istanbul, Turkey, Rifat Ozbek (1953–) moved to the UK in the 1970s. Initially, he studied architecture at the University of Liverpool, but soon transferred to Saint Martins School of Art to enrol on a fashion course. He graduated in 1977 and, after a stint in Italy and another with high-street clothing chain Monsoon, launched his own label in 1984, showing out of his parents' apartment in Belgravia.

The British fashion renaissance of the 1980s was more about creative idealism than industry domination. Life at his studio in Haunch of Venison Yard, in London's Mayfair, was as much about 'the happening' as building a business. His eclectic, romantic style drew on influences as disparate as the actress Juliette Greco, choreographer Martha Graham and the mariachi musicians of South America, and attracted the attention of some stylish heavy hitters such as Tina Chow, Grace Coddington and Polly Mellen, who were among the young designer's earliest supporters. In a fashion world obsessed with streetwear and minimalism, he offered a unique and global point of view, using rich and exotic fabric combinations – prints from Africa, silks from the Far East, raffia from Spain and woven cloth from South America.

The Ozbek look became known for its vibrant colour palette and rich textiles. He was comfortable styling glossy Venetian wools along with tribal ikat fabrics. He dressed sarong skirts up with city coats and accessorized evening dresses with a Turkish fez. An Ozbek collection was a visual feast that also managed to translate from the catwalk to real women's wardrobes.

An Ozbek ensemble from Spring/Summer 1988. Rifat Ozbek introduced a cosmopolitan *joie de vivre* into what was fast becoming a tired London fashion scene.

ARTHUR ELGORT

Energizing fashion photographer

At the heart of an Elgort image is the captured moment: a spontaneous freshness that belies the painstaking attention to detail that goes into the set-up of each shot. Elgort's (1940–) first job was as an usher working at Carnegie Hall where he fell in love with dance. He took pictures of George Balanchine and the New York City Ballet, and central to his style has always been his love of unfettered and graceful movement. 'Move with your subject' is a piece of advice he has often offered to aspiring photographers.

While working for American *Vogue*, he exploited the potential of their lavish production budgets to the full, travelling to increasingly exotic locations and bringing a cinematic dimension to his fashion spreads. But what made him unique, however, was his ability to portray an intimacy within the grand scale. Women do tend to relax around Elgort, and that has been key to many of his most memorable images. He catches them backstage, during downtime, on the phone, with hair in curlers, smoking, in any level of undress. 'I always feel that it's a compliment when a woman reveals herself in front of the camera,' he wrote in his 1993 book *Arthur Elgort's Models Manual*. 'It shows she trusts me. That's what a good picture is all about.'

Elgort's iconic 'snapshot' style transformed the fashion landscape in the 1970s and 1980s, and he remains one of the most inspiring (and imitated) lensmen working today. 'You can take a picture or you can make a picture. I much prefer the latter,' Elgort told *Vogue* in 1989.

Linda Evangelista as shot by Arthur Elgort in 1989. Elgort's images are always full of motion.

JOHN GALLIANO

English dreamer

John Galliano (1960–) graduated from Saint Martins School of Art in 1984 at the height of London's hedonistic decade. At that time, the Saint Martins campus bordered the heart of clubland. Young London lived to dress up, and the nights were a peacock parade led by larger-than-life characters such as Leigh Bowery and Boy George. Galliano remembered how 'Thursday and Friday the college was almost deserted. Everybody was at home working on their costumes for the weekend.'

It was a time of outrage. And London was the perfect crucible for Galliano's rare imagination. His graduate collection, 'Les Incroyables', was fired by the flamboyance of the New Romantic club scene and driven by his determination to change the architecture of fashion – how it was cut, assembled and worn. With his ability to marshal a kaleidoscopic range of influences – a skill that was to define his work throughout his career – he also sought to capture the creativity and innocence of children. He was fascinated by how they dressed themselves haphazardly, with legs through armholes and arms through necks. 'It's all a mad mix,' Galliano explained. 'Everything is off balance. I break every possible rule and find different looks emerge by playing with how they are put on the body – fashion has never been so exciting.'

Working with Amanda Grieve, fashion editor at *Harpers & Queen*, Galliano became a London Fashion Week star with a succession of inventive, gorgeous and exorbitantly uneconomical collections. With visionary ideas but little business sense, he went bankrupt in 1990, a fitting end to the decade of excess.

An illustration by Howard Tangye showing a model wearing a Galliano hat and coat. The image captures the flamboyant Galliano silhouette of the late 1980s.

HERB RITTS

Athletic glamour

Son of a successful entrepreneur, Herb Ritts (1952–2002) grew up in LA in the 1960s and '70s. His next-door neighbours were Steve McQueen and his wife, and as a child he would entertain the starry couple with puppet shows. In his twenties he became friends with a crowd of rising actors and musicians, who gravitated to the city: people like Richard Gere and Elton John and the cast of the *Rocky Horror Picture Show*. It was during these formative years that Ritts honed one of his trademark skills – making famous people feel at their ease. It was a skill that he would need on a daily basis as contributor to *Vogue*, *Vanity Fair* and *Rolling Stone* over the following twenty years.

In the beginning Ritts simply toyed with a camera using his friends as subjects. He was drawn to the style of Hurrell, Man Ray and Horst, masters of light and strong classical lines. He followed in the footsteps of Robert Mapplethorpe and Bruce Weber (see page 26) in his fascination with the human form. But it was his familiarity with the California landscape, its light and seascapes, that really opened up his visual vocabulary and allowed him to create a truly modern style. It was this strong and harsh light that became his signature,
a key, he felt, to unlocking a dynamic life force within his subjects.

In a decade defined by artifice, he created an anti-glamour style, taking his subjects out of the studio and into natural light. It was the era when no glossy magazine was complete without Naomi Campbell, Claudia Schiffer, Christy Turlington, Linda Evangelista or Tatjana Patitz. It was Ritts who arguably mythologized these Amazonian beauties and elevated them to a new status – that of supermodel. There was a current of sensuality running through all of Ritts's work, but it was always heroic rather than trivial. His iconic image of a quintet of naked supermodels, limbs intertwined (1989), manages to be about strength, elegance and poise rather than titillation.

Tatjana Patitz, as shot by Herb Ritts in Hollywood, 1989. It was through such iconic images that Ritts helped forge the mythology of the supermodel in the late 1980s.

JOSEPH
A fashion essential

Joseph Ettedgui (1936–2010), son of a shopkeeper from Casablanca, forged his first career in London as a hairdresser, but in the 1980s redefined fashion retailing. In the postmodern age, fashion designers made chairs and furnishing fabrics and world-famous architects designed clothes shops. Ettedgui pioneered the selling of furniture and ceramics side by side with frocks and became the beating heart of London's glamorous new brand of cool.

In the wake of the deregulation of the financial markets in 1986, The Joseph store on Brompton Road (designed by Norman Foster) was the mecca for the newly style-conscious and newly rich. There, the customers could immerse themselves in two splendid floors of Ettedgui's meticulously curated selection of the best of catwalk fashion. No designer, anywhere in the world, could consider themselves to have made it until they were stocked by Joseph. Here the customer could browse the Gallianos and Gaultiers, swaddle themselves in statement sweaters from Joseph Tricot, and kit themselves out in 'basics' from his eponymous label.

Ettedgui brought the cool modernism of France to the UK. Subscribing very much to Andrée Puttman's view that 'We are suffering from an overdose of colour', he wore only black in winter and only white in summer. By the end of the 1980s this asceticism was universal. Women in black sweaters, tight black pants and flat black ballerinas climbed into small black cars and drove home to minimalist black and chrome apartments. They wrote with fat black pens and put on black dresses to dance to black music in black clubs. Black was the only fashionable colour ... and Joseph was the mecca of monochrome.

A Joseph advertisement from the late 1980s. Crisp silhouettes and ubiquitous black were hallmarks of the Joseph style.

ROMEO GIGLI

Fashion's faerie prince

1989

Romeo Gigli (1949–), an architect by training, showed his first fashion collection in Milan in 1985. Two retailing visionaries snapped it up: Joan Burstein of Browns, London, and Joyce Ma of the eponymous boutique in Hong Kong. By the end of the decade Gigli had moved his shows to Paris and had achieved superstar status, hailed as 'a fashion game-changer, the Armani of the '90s'.

In stark contrast to the power dressing and body-conscious clothes that dominated the runways, his style was an uncompromising vision of romantic individualism. His proposal was more like a fashion dream sequence than a sartorial passport to the boardroom: rhapsodic designs in rare fabrics, a rich palette of Indian spice colours and a treasure trove of cultural references. In Gigli's hands, fashion was approaching the realm of art.

The Gigli silhouette consisted of shawl-collar necklines, small unpadded shoulders, bandeau-swathed bodices and empire waistlines. Long, slim sleeves reached over the fingertips. Sensual velvets, diaphanous organzas, delicate silks and rich brocades, in gorgeous jewel tones, all harked back to the riches of the Renaissance. A Gigli show was, as one critic described it, replete with a 'luxury worthy of an Eastern potentate. So lavish were his designs, so intricate his embroideries…'

Such eclectic, historical and otherworldly references do not sound like a recipe for success in the late twentieth century and, yet, his star status was assured because he also managed to be pre-eminently modern in those romantic silhouettes.

A fashion model wears a ready-to-wear off-the-shoulder blouse and ruffled skirt by Romeo Gigli. Gigli's clothes were both lavish and intellectual, combining a sensuality of form and texture with a wide range of cultural and conceptual references.

INDEX

PICTURE CREDITS

The publisher would like to thank the following contributors for their kind permission to reproduce the following photographs:

2 Brendan Beirne/Rex Features; 4 Dianna; 5 below Ferdinando Scianna/Magnum Photos; above Janette Beckman/PYMCA.com 7 Alan Davidson/The Picture Library Ltd; 8 Yoram Kahana/Rex Features; 9 Everett Collection/Rex Features; 11 Rose Hartman/Getty Images; 13 Jean-Paul Goude; 15 Courtesy of Prada; 17 Marilynn K. Yee/The New York Times/Redux/Eyevine; 19 Moviestore Collection/Rex Features; 21 Bettmann/Corbis; 22 Ted Polhemus/PYMCA.com; 25 Courtesy of Vinmags; 27 Bettmann/Corbis; 29 below Contrasto/Eyevine above Olycom SPA/Rex Features; 31 Daniel Simon/Gamma-Rapho via Getty Images; 33 London Features International; 35 Denis Piel/Conde Nast Archive/Corbis; 37 Andrea Blanch/Hulton Archive/Getty Images; 39 Jayne Fincher/Princess Diana Archive/Getty Images; 41 Thomas Iannaccone/Condé Nast Archive/Corbis; 43 Thomas Iannaccone/Conde Nast Archive/Corbis; 43 ITV/Rex Features; 45 L.J.van Houten/Rex Features; 47 Judy Montgomery/Courtesy of Bodymap; 48 Richard Kalvar/Magnum Photos; 49 Pierre Vauthey/Sygma/Corbis; 51 PA Archive/Press Association Images; 53 David Mcgough/DMI/Time Life Pictures/Getty Images; 55 Universal/Everett/Rex Features; 57 Lyn Goldsmith/Rex Features; 59 Ebet Robert/Redferns/Getty Images; 61 David Montgomery/Hulton Archive/ Getty Images; 63 Chris Moore/Catwalking; 65 Sharok Hatami/Rex Features; 67 Universal/Everett/Rex Features; 69 Harry Langdon/Getty Images; 70 Lars Pehrson/Scanpic/Press Association; 71 Jamie Morgan; 73 Glen E. Friedman; 74 Richard Young/Rex Features; 75 Brendan Beirne/Rex Features; 76 David Montgomery/Hulton Archive/Getty Images; 77 Duncan Raban/EMPICS Entertainment; 79 Chris Moore/Catwalking; 81 Anthea Sims; 83 Richard Young/Rex Features; 85 Everett Collection/Rex Features; 87 Ebet Roberts/Redferns/Getty Images; 89 Nick Knight/Trunk Archive 91 Ian Cook/Time & Life Pictures/Getty Images; 93 Brian Rasic/Rex Features; 95 Kobal 97 Chris Moore/Catwalking; 99 Arthur Elgort; 101 Howard Tangye 103 Herb Ritts/Trunk Archive; 105 Courtesy of Joseph; 107 Pierre Vauthey/Sygma/Corbis

Every effort has been made to trace the copyright holders. We apologise in advance for any unintentional omissions and would be pleased to insert the appropriate acknowledgement in any subsequent publication.

First published in 2013
by Conran Octopus Ltd
a part of Octopus Publishing
Group, Endeavour House,
189 Shaftesbury Avenue,
London WC2H 8JY
www.octopusbooks.co.uk

An Hachette UK Company
www.hachette.co.uk

Distributed in the US by
Hachette Book Group USA,
237 Park Avenue, New York,
NY 10017 USA

Distributed in Canada by
Canadian Manda Group,
165 Dufferin Street, Toronto,
Ontario, Canada M6K 3H6

British Library Cataloguing-
in-Publication Data.
A catalogue record for this
book is available from the
British Library.

Text written by: Paula Reed

Publisher: Alison Starling
Consultant Editor:
Deyan Sudjic
Senior Editor:
Sybella Stephens
Editor: Robert Anderson
Design: Untitled
Picture Research:
Sara Rumens
Production Controller:
Sarah Kramer

ISBN: 978 1 84091 626 3
Printed in China